A Dangerous Game

JANET LORIMER

GLOBE FEARON
Pearson Learning Group

DOUBLE FASTBACK® SPY BOOKS

Against the Wall
The Black Gold Conspiracy
Claw the Cold, Cold Earth
A Dangerous Game
Escape From East Berlin

The Last Red Rose
Picture of Evil
The Puppeteer
The Race to Ross
The Silver Spy

Cover © Corbis. All photography © Pearson Education, Inc. (PEI) unless specifically noted.

Copyright © 2004 by Pearson Education, Inc., publishing as Globe Fearon®, an imprint of Pearson Learning Group, 299 Jefferson Road, Parsippany, NJ 07054. All rights reserved. No part of this book may be reproduced or transmitted in any form or by any means, electronic or mechanical, including photocopying, recording, or by any information storage and retrieval system, without permission in writing from the publisher. For information regarding permission(s), write to Rights and Permissions Department.

Globe Fearon® and Fastback® are registered trademarks of Globe Fearon, Inc.

ISBN 0-13-024621-2
Printed in the United States of America
1 2 3 4 5 6 7 8 9 10   07 06 05 04 03

Globe Fearon
Pearson Learning Group

1-800-321-3106
www.pearsonlearning.com

Don't give up! Don't give up! You're almost there!

The words went round and round inside Pam's head. She forced herself to say them over and over as her body cut through the cold water. It was a trick she had taught herself when she first began swimming. She wouldn't let herself think about how far she had to go, or how much her muscles ached.

Pam's fingers touched the wall of the pool. She reached up and grabbed the edge.

For a moment she held onto the tile, resting her tired body. Then she pulled herself out of the pool.

Her swimming coach, Don Holland, handed her a towel. "How did I do?" she asked, as she wiped her face.

The wide grin on his face told her everything. "You came very close to breaking your own record, Pam. It won't be long before you're ready for some long distance swimming. These practice sessions are really paying off."

Pam grinned back. She was tired and sore, but it was worth it.

"You'd better go get changed," Holland told her. "I'll see you here next Saturday."

As Pam headed for the showers, a man came up to her and said, "Excuse me. Are you Pam Norton?"

Pam nodded, wondering how he knew her name. He was a short stocky man with dark hair. She had never seen him before.

"My name is Frank Dawson," he said. "I'm a friend of your sister's."

"Trish?" Pam said in surprise.

Dawson nodded. "Trish asked me to get in touch with you. She's had an accident." Then, seeing the look on Pam's face, he added quickly, "But don't worry. She's going to be fine."

"What happened to her?" Pam said.

"She was skiing in Italy," Dawson said. "She fell and broke her leg."

Pam stared at him in disbelief. "My sister on skis? Trish hates sports!"

Dawson smiled. "Yes, I know. But she'd just met a good-looking ski instructor and she was trying to impress him."

Pam laughed. "Yes, that sounds like Trish," she said. "Can you tell me what hospital she's in? I'd like to get in touch with her."

"Sure," Dawson said. "But why don't you change out of that wet suit first. I'll meet you in the coffee shop next door and then we can talk. All right?"

"All right," Pam said. She started to walk away, but Dawson's next words made her stop.

"I can't get over how much you and Trish look alike," he said. "You look almost like twins."

"That's what everyone says," Pam said. "But I'm a year younger than Trish. And we're really very different people."

Dawson nodded, but Pam had a strange feeling that he hadn't really heard what she'd said.

While she was changing, Pam thought about Trish. She and her sister did look alike. Both had curly brown hair and green eyes. Both had wide smiles with dimples. Both were tall and thin.

But in other ways the sisters were quite different. Trish was the outgoing one. She loved excitement. Trish worked as an airline flight attendant. When she wasn't working, she was usually partying.

Pam, on the other hand, was quiet and shy. She worked in a bank. On weekends she swam at the health club. She loved sports, but most of all swimming.

Because they had such different interests, the sisters didn't see each other very often. Trish traveled so much anyway. Pam hadn't talked to her for several weeks. She thought about Trish with a cast on her leg, and she couldn't help smiling a little.

"Serves her right for trying to pretend to be a skier just to impress some man," Pam thought.

Dawson was waiting at a table in the coffee shop. After Pam ordered a cup of coffee, he said, "I work for the Federal Bureau of Investigation, Pam."

Dawson said it so casually that it took Pam a few seconds to understand what he had said. "The FBI?" she said, a little puzzled.

Dawson nodded. "How do you know my sister?" Pam asked.

"Let me explain," Dawson said. "Trish was about to do a job for us when she broke her leg."

Pam stared at him. "Are you saying my sister works for the FBI?" she gasped in disbelief. "But I thought—"

"—that she worked for an airline," Dawson finished. "She does. Actually, Trish was only going to do one job for us."

"I don't understand," Pam said.

"Maybe I should start at the beginning," Dawson said. "Did you ever hear of a man named Alexander Cameron?"

Pam frowned. "The name sounds familiar. Isn't he an extremely wealthy man? I think I've seen his name in the newspaper."

Dawson nodded. "That's right. Cameron is a billionaire. He's also a man with some very dangerous ideas about politics and world power. He believes there's only one way that the United States can stay powerful. And that is if we stop talking about peace and start taking action against our enemies."

"Action?" Pam said. "You mean, like war?"

Dawson nodded. "For the last two years, Cameron has been gathering a lot of dangerous men together. Men who think the way he does. Cameron is building his own army."

"Isn't that against the law?" Pam asked.

Dawson shook his head. "Cameron makes sure he does everything within the law," he said. "So far, we haven't been able to touch him because he's been so careful. However, we have reason to believe that he's planning to do something with that army of his very soon."

"Why do you say that?" Pam asked.

"Cameron has a huge estate on the island of Oahu in Hawaii. He's been moving his people to Oahu for the last few weeks. The men have been arriving there in small groups. They act like tourists, but we know they aren't. Once they arrive on Oahu, they all head for Cameron's estate. We're pretty sure he's been smuggling in guns, too. But we have no way to prove it. That estate is well guarded. One of our people tried to secretly get into Cameron's army. But his real identity was discovered before he could learn anything that would help us. After that, Cameron tightened his security even more. Now his estate is like a fortress."

Pam shuddered. "Cameron sounds crazy," she said.

"Crazy and dangerous," Dawson said. "We have to find out what he's up to before he does something with that army of his."

"Like what?" Pam asked.

Dawson shrugged. "We aren't sure. Like I said, we can't get close enough to him to find out. But he has said over and over again that the United States should launch an all-out attack on its enemies—instead of talking about peace."

Pam stared at Dawson in horror. "That could start another world war," she said.

"Right," Dawson said. "That's why we have to stop Cameron before he goes too far with his plan."

"What does all this have to do with my sister?" Pam asked.

"About three weeks ago, Trish met Cameron at a party in Los Angeles. He was completely charmed by her. You know what a bubbly personality Trish has. Before the evening was over, Cameron invited her to come to his estate in Hawaii. He's going to have a few friends in for a weekend house party. Trish accepted the invitation.

"One of our people overheard Cameron talking to Trish. When I found out that she'd been invited to his estate, I got in touch with her right away. I told her what I've told you. I asked her if she would be willing to help us learn more about Cameron's plans."

"And she agreed?" Pam asked.

"Yes. The idea of playing 'secret agent' really appealed to her," Dawson said. "To be honest, we don't like to use people who aren't professionals. But it seemed to us that Trish was our only hope. When she said she would help us, we began to give her a crash course for this job. Then she broke her leg. Now it will be impossible for her to go to Cameron's party."

"I'm sorry to hear that," Pam said. "I guess you must be pretty disappointed."

"Not just disappointed," Dawson said. "Worried, too. As I said, Trish was our only hope. I'm convinced that Cameron and his men are going to act soon."

Pam nodded. "I understand how you must feel. But I don't see why you're telling me all this. There's nothing I can do to help you. I—"

All of a sudden she stared at Dawson, her eyes growing wide. Now she understood why he had been interested in the likeness between herself and Trish! "You aren't thinking that—" she said.

Dawson nodded. "When Trish broke her leg, I figured that was that. We'd lost our chance of ever finding out what Cameron is up to before he makes his move. Then I remembered that when I had done a check of Trish's background, there was information about her having a younger sister. And when I checked *your* background I realized you look enough like her to be her twin. That's right, Pam. We want you to pretend you're Trish and go to that party."

Pam didn't know how long she stared at Frank Dawson. He couldn't be serious. But from the look on his face, she knew that he was.

"That's impossible!" she said finally. "I couldn't do it."

"When I talked to Trish about this, she told me that sometimes you changed places and pretended to be each other," he said.

Pam laughed. "Oh, sure, years ago when we were in high school. It was kind of a game back then. Usually it was Trish's idea. She loved to fool people. But that was a long time ago, Mr. Dawson. Trish and I are quite different now. We don't dress the same. She wears her hair short, and mine is long. Our interests, our whole lives, are very different now."

"Getting you to look like Trish wouldn't be hard," Dawson said slowly. "We can have your hair cut to look just like hers. You can wear her clothes and—"

"Hold it!" Pam said. "You just don't understand. We have very different personalities. I couldn't fool anyone who has met Trish into believing I'm her."

"You did it before in high school," Dawson said. "You could practice."

Pam stared at him in frustration. "Even if I did look and act like Trish, that would only be a small part of it. I'm not a secret agent! I'm a bank teller! I don't know the first thing about spying. And that's what you want me to do."

"We can train you," Dawson said.

"But—" Just the thought of sneaking around Cameron's estate scared her. "You don't understand," she said again. There was a note of panic in her voice now. "When Trish and I changed places in high school, it was a silly game. This would be a very *dangerous* one."

Dawson sighed. This time he didn't have a quick answer. "Yes, you're right," he said. "It would be dangerous."

"I can't do it," Pam said firmly. "I'm sorry, Mr. Dawson but I'd be scared to death. I'd never get away with it. I don't know why Trish ever suggested such a thing to you."

"Well, to be honest, she didn't," Dawson said slowly. "In fact, she was against the idea."

"She was?" Pam said.

"She said you'd never do anything more dangerous than cross a busy street against a red light," Dawson said. His face flushed a little as he spoke.

"That's what she said?" Pam said angrily. Her face turned red. She could almost hear Trish laughing at the idea of Pam working for the FBI.

"I can't blame you for not wanting to get involved," Dawson went on. "Even though we'd do everything to get you ready, once you were inside Cameron's estate, you'd be on your own. I told you that Trish thought it would be exciting. But that's Trish. I can see you're a much quieter, more thoughtful person."

"Trish loves adventure," Pam said. "She wouldn't think twice about taking chances. That's why she'd be much better for this job than I would."

"No, I don't think so," Dawson said. "I think you're better suited for this job than your sister."

"Me?" Pam said in surprise. "Why?"

"Because you're more serious. You'd be more careful. I'm afraid Trish might have taken too many risks. We were willing to use her because we didn't have much choice. But this job calls for someone with a cool head. Please, Pam, won't you reconsider?"

Pam bit her lower lip. Dawson's words made her feel a little better, but she still couldn't imagine herself as a spy. "What will you do if I say no?" she asked.

"I don't know what we'll do," Dawson said. "Time is running out. You're just about our last hope!"

"But if you don't find a way to stop Cameron," she said, "he might—" She couldn't go on.

Dawson looked at Pam steadily. "Look, Pam, as I told you before, I don't like using untrained people. I really wish we could send in one of our own agents. But we can't get anyone in. If you do help us, you'll be taking a big risk. On the other hand, you may be the one person right now who can save your country from possibly being plunged into war."

Pam swallowed hard. Her mouth felt dry, but the palms of her hands were cold and damp. She had always tried to be a good citizen. But she never thought she'd be asked to do something like this for her country.

"Oh, I don't know what to tell you," she groaned. "I hate to let you down. But it seems so scary and—" She stopped and took a deep breath. "Can I have a few days to think it over?" she asked.

Dawson shook his head. "When I said that time was running out, I meant it. Cameron's party is next weekend. You'll have to make a decision right away."

Pam sighed, not knowing what to say. Then she thought about how she'd envied Trish for almost her entire life. Pam had often wished she could be as outgoing as her older sister. She felt hurt whenever Trish teased her about her quiet life and her dull job at the bank. And now Trish was certain that Pam wouldn't be able to do something dangerous, even to help her country.

Trish was always so sure that she knew what Pam would do and say. Suddenly Pam's resentment came to the surface. Maybe it was time she proved to Trish, and herself, that she wasn't a shy little mouse!

"I'll do it," she heard herself say.

During the next few days, Pam almost believed the whole thing was a crazy dream. Sometimes she thought that if she pinched herself, she'd wake up and find herself back in the bank. Or at the swimming pool. Instead, her quiet, well-planned world had been turned upside down.

Pam's training began almost from the moment she agreed to work for Dawson. First she was made to look exactly like Trish. Her hair was cut and styled in the same way. She was given Trish's clothes. She practiced walking and talking like her sister. By the third day, Dawson said, "I think you have a hidden talent, Pam. You'd make a great actress. If I didn't know better, I would think that you are Trish Norton!"

"But will Alexander Cameron?" Pam said. "He's the one I have to fool."

"Don't worry," Dawson told her. "Cameron only spent a few hours with

Trish. He doesn't know her that well. You won't have any trouble fooling him."

Pretending to be Trish was the easy part. Pam also had to study pictures of Alexander Cameron as well as floor plans of his huge house.

"The house was built long before Cameron bought the estate," Dawson said. "So we were able to get the floor plans. We know what some of the rooms are being used for. But we can only guess which one might be Cameron's office. And that's probably where you'll find the information we want."

"I can't just walk into his office and start going through his desk," Pam said.

"That's right," Dawson told her. "First you'll have to find it. Then you'll have to figure out a way to get into it. It may be kept locked and guarded. We just don't know. And we aren't even sure what you should look for once you get inside."

Pam groaned. "And all this has to be done in three days," she said.

Dawson nodded. "I didn't say it would be easy."

By the end of the week, Pam was as ready as she could be. She'd packed her suitcase and was waiting for Dawson to take her to the airport. In a couple of hours she'd be on a plane heading for Oahu.

Just before Dawson took her to the airport, he gave her a small box. "Open it," he said. "There's something in it for you."

Pam opened it and looked inside. A pair of pearl earrings lay in the box. "They're beautiful," she said.

"They're more than beautiful," Dawson told her. "They could save your life. One of them contains a tiny transmitter. When you press the pearl, it will send a signal to me. I'll be on Oahu the whole time and as close to the estate as I can get. If I get your signal, I'll know you're in danger."

I'm glad I had my ears pierced, Pam thought as she removed her little silver studs and replaced them with the pearl set. "OK, they're on," she said.

Dawson patted her shoulder. "You're going to be just fine," he told her. "After it's all over, you can go back to your job at the bank as if nothing had ever happened."

"I don't think so," Pam said. "I have a funny feeling that my life is never going to be quite the same again. That is, if I get out of this alive!"

"Just keep your eyes and ears open," Dawson reminded her. "Don't take any unnecessary chances. And don't underestimate Cameron. He's a very powerful, very dangerous man."

Several hours later, Pam's plane landed on Oahu. When she stepped off the plane, she was met by one of Cameron's men. He introduced himself as David Owens. Although he was very polite, he never smiled. Pam noticed a suspicious bulge under his jacket. Was it a gun? She tried to hide a small shiver of fear.

When they reached Cameron's estate, Pam saw that the place was well guarded. Men and dogs were on patrol in front of the high walls. As the huge gates clanged shut behind her, Pam shivered again.

Cameron was standing on the wide front steps when the limousine rolled to a stop. He opened the door himself and helped her out. He was a tall man in his fifties with gray hair and dark eyes. And although he seemed pleasant enough, Pam felt that behind his smile there was something hard and cold.

"How was your trip?" he asked as they went into the house.

"Oh, wonderful," Pam said in a bubbly Trish voice. "You know how much I love to fly!" She laughed the way Trish would have laughed. Cameron smiled.

"I'll have my housekeeper show you to your room," he said. "Then you can meet my other guests."

The housekeeper was a middle-aged Hawaiian woman named Lehua. She took Pam's suitcase and asked Pam to follow her up the main staircase.

Pam thought she had never seen such a big and beautiful house. It had been built to be kept as cool as possible in the warm Hawaiian climate. The floors were polished wood, and the furniture was made of rattan. There were bowls of bright flowers everywhere. Even though Pam had studied plans of the house, she was still surprised by how big it was. There were several floors. Hallways led to other hallways, each connecting many rooms. She knew that finding Cameron's office would not be easy.

Lehua showed Pam to a large, comfortable bedroom with its own bathroom. She offered to unpack Pam's suitcase, but Pam said she would rather do it herself. Lehua did not seem to want to leave. She straightened the pillows on the bed and wiped away some dust on the dressing table and nearby chair.

"This house is very large," Lehua said at last. "Are you sure you can find your way back downstairs? I would be happy to wait and take you down myself."

Her meaning was very clear. Lehua did not want Pam wandering around on her own. Pam wondered why. Surely the housekeeper did not suspect her. Perhaps all of Cameron's guests were being treated the same way.

"Goodness," Pam laughed. "I'm not a child, Lehua. I won't get lost."

"All right, miss," Lehua said. She left the room with a stern look on her face.

Pam unpacked and changed into shorts and a cool top. Then she hurried into the hall and began opening doors, one by one. There were so many rooms on this one floor that it took her quite a while to search them. When she was done, she discovered that they were all bedrooms. The office must be on another floor. She knew she had wasted time, but it had been necessary. She hurried down to the next floor.

She was about to open the first door she came to, when the door suddenly opened. David Owens stepped into the hall. For a moment they just stared at each other in surprise. Then David said, "What are you doing here?"

Pam tried to cover her panic by acting just like Trish would have. "Goodness, Mr. Owens, you startled me! But I'm so glad to see you. I'm hopelessly lost! How in the world do I get downstairs?"

David frowned. "The stairs are right there, Miss Norton."

Pam waved his answer aside. "I was looking for an elevator," she said impatiently. "Surely Alexander doesn't expect people to climb those stairs all the time. Goodness, I'll feel like a mountain goat before the weekend is over!"

Owens gritted his teeth. "I'm sorry, Miss Norton, there is no elevator. And you just can't wander around on your own like this."

She flashed a big smile at him, hoping to charm him. "Oh, David, you don't think I'm going to run off with the family jewels, do you? Really!"

She had hoped to trick him into telling her why parts of this house were off-limits. But the trick failed. Owens politely, but firmly, escorted her down to the patio.

Cameron and his guests were sitting on the wide stone patio enjoying the cool breeze. When Pam arrived, Cameron introduced her to the others. They were all older than she was. All of them seemed to be wealthy friends of Cameron's. They seemed to know each other very well, and they didn't seem interested in Pam. When everyone was seated again, Lehua brought out frosty glasses of iced tea for everyone.

As she sipped her cool drink, Pam said to Cameron, "I love your house, Alexander. It's very grand! I do hope you'll give me a guided tour."

Cameron smiled. "Of course, my dear," he said. "But first I want to show you the outside. I think you'll enjoy the gardens. I have a greenhouse filled with tropical flowers. There's also the swimming pool and the stables, in case you'd like to go horseback riding. And I have tennis courts, too. I'm sure you'll find a lot to keep you busy this weekend."

Pam pretended to pout a little. She had remembered, just in time, that Trish could not swim and did not care much for the other activities. "But Alexander, you know I don't like outdoor sports very much. I was hoping that you and I would be able to go sightseeing."

"I'm afraid that something has come up that will keep me busy all weekend," he said slowly. "But I'm sure you'll find enough to keep you busy during the day. And in the evening we'll have some time together. I have a game room, you know. And don't forget, when I invited you, you promised to be a fourth for bridge."

For a second, Pam nearly panicked. Bridge? She had never played that card game in her life! And she didn't realize that Trish knew how to play. How was she going to get out of this one?

At that moment, Lehua hurried out to the patio. She came to tell Cameron that he had a phone call. He nodded and stood up. "Excuse me, Trish, but this is business. Business before pleasure. You understand."

Pam flashed a big smile at him. It was important for Cameron to like her. That way she could get away with more. "Don't worry about me," she said. "I'll be all right on my own."

Cameron smiled back, and he hurried away to take his call. Pam took a deep breath. The other guests were busy talking. They paid no attention to her. She got up and strolled away.

The grounds of the estate were beautiful. There were broad green lawns and lovely flower gardens. She soon found the pool, tennis courts, and stables. She kept wandering farther and farther from the house. She hoped that if anyone were watching, it would look as if she were just out for a walk. But as she walked, her mind raced.

She was sure that something had come up this weekend, something that had forced Cameron to put his business before his party. Could it be that he was getting ready to make his move very soon? After all, Dawson had said the army was already gathering somewhere on the estate.

Suddenly Pam heard a sound that startled her. It sounded like gunshots. Ahead was a grove of trees. The sounds seemed to have come from that direction. Pam strolled to the grove and followed a narrow pathway through the trees. Now she could hear other sounds. There were men's voices and the noise of engines.

When Pam reached the far side of the grove, she stepped quickly behind a tree. Ahead was a large field. There was a long line of buildings that looked like army barracks. Men in green army fatigues hurried in all directions. Pam saw jeeps and trucks parked in front of the buildings. Men were loading large wooden crates onto the trucks. And, she saw that Dawson had been right about the guns. Several men were firing at paper targets.

Cameron's army! And from the looks of it, they were getting ready to go somewhere and do something. But what? And when? And where? This was the information Dawson needed. She knew she had to find it as soon as possible.

Suddenly, she felt a hand clamp down on her arm. She cried out in fear and surprise.

It was David Owens. And he was very angry. "What are you doing here?" he snapped.

Pam thought quickly as she tried to pull her arm free. Trish would never let anyone talk to her like that. She glared at David. "How dare you sneak up behind me like that!" she exclaimed. "Take your hand off me, right now!"

Her reaction surprised him. He let go of her arm, but he was still angry. "You have no business being out here," he said. "Does Mr. Cameron know—"

Pam cut him off. "I was out for a walk," she said crossly. "Alexander had a business call, and I was left all alone. I must say, Mr. Owens, this is no way to treat a houseguest."

Owens took a deep breath to get his temper under control. "I'm sorry, Miss

Norton. I thought you knew that there were places on the estate where you must not go."

"Well, I didn't," Pam snapped, pushing past him. "I've a good mind to pack my suitcase and leave right now. I'm not used to being treated like this. So far this is the most boring house party I've ever been to!"

"Why don't you go for a swim?" Owens said. He was trying to calm her down. Part of his job, Pam guessed, was trying to keep Cameron's guests happy. "Or maybe you'd like to go riding," he added. "One of Mr. Cameron's men would be happy to go with you."

Pam sighed. "No, thank you," she said. "I can't swim, if you must know, and I'm not fond of horses. I think I'll just go up to my room and read a magazine. Unless reading is off-limits, too!"

Owens winced. "Look, Miss Norton, I'm very sorry about all this." He kept talking, trying to calm her down and make her feel better. But Pam was only half-listening. By now they had reached the back of the house. Pam saw something that made her blink with surprise. Two windows on the first floor had bars on the outside. The room inside must be very special. In fact, she was willing to bet that that was Cameron's office.

When they reached the patio, Owens tried one last time to apologize. Pam turned to him and smiled a little. "I forgive you for scaring me like that," she said, cutting into his words. "And I won't say a word to Alexander. It will be our little secret."

Owens took another deep breath. Pam wasn't sure if he was trying to swallow his anger, or if he was relieved. Either way, she wanted him to think that she was a silly, empty-headed woman. It was the only way she thought he would not suspect her of being nosy.

Owens hurried away on business of his own. The other guests had left the patio. Pam glanced at her watch. It was nearly four o'clock. The others were probably resting before dinner or changing their clothes. If the staff was busy preparing dinner, this would be a good time to do some snooping inside the house. And if anyone stopped her, she had her excuse all ready.

Pam walked into the main hall. There were many rooms leading off it, including a large living room, a dining room, and the game room. Beyond the dining room would be the kitchen. Straight ahead Pam saw a set of double doors. They looked like they might be the doors leading into the room with barred windows. She took a deep breath and hurried across the hall. She tried the handle, but the doors were locked. That didn't surprise her. She was sure this must be the right room.

"What are you doing, miss?"

Pam turned quickly. Lehua was standing behind her. She was holding a tray with a coffee pot and cups on it. And from one hand dangled a key ring.

"Oh, Lehua, you're just the person I need. I'm trying to find a magazine. But the library seems to be locked."

"That's not the library," Lehua said. "The library is over there." She nodded in another direction.

"Goodness," Pam said in her Trish-like voice. "A person needs a *map* to get around this place."

Lehua set the tray down on a table near the locked doors. "I'll take you to the library," she said.

"Oh, never mind," Pam said. "I can find it myself now." As she crossed the hall to the library, she could feel Lehua watching her. As soon as Pam was inside the library, she closed the door. She waited for a moment, and then she opened it a crack.

She watched Lehua unlock the double doors, pick up the tray and disappear inside. At that moment, a group of men came into the main hall. Pam saw Cameron, David Owens, and several men in green fatigues. They, too, disappeared into the same room. Then Lehua came out and hurried off toward the kitchen.

When the hall was empty, Pam slipped out and hurried up to her room. She would have loved to have pressed her ear against those doors to hear what those men were saying. But it was too big a risk. Still, she was making progress. Now she was sure she had found Cameron's office. All she had to do next was get inside.

Pam showered and changed for dinner. She chose a cream-colored silk evening dress that she was sure Cameron would like. While she was dressing, she was thinking of a way to get into his office. Lehua had a key on that key ring. Where would she keep it? Probably someplace in the kitchen where she could grab it if she were in a hurry.

Just as Pam was getting ready to go downstairs, there was a knock on her door. She opened it and saw Alexander Cameron in the hall. His eyes widened with pleasure when he looked at her.

"You look *beautiful*, Trish," he said.

"Why thank you, Alexander," Pam said sweetly.

"May I escort you to the dining room?" he said, taking her arm.

All through dinner, Pam kept up a light flow of bright chatter. She played Trish at her best. She was amusing and charming and she saw that Cameron was pleased.

After dinner, he said, "Well, Trish, what about that game of bridge?"

Pam had completely forgotten about it. She felt a small stab of panic. She smiled at Cameron, but she quickly tried to figure a way out. She pretended to stifle a big yawn. "Oh, Alexander, I'm just so tired. Couldn't we put it off till tomorrow? After all, I don't want you to win too easily." She smiled up at him in a flirting way from under her eyelashes.

Cameron grinned. "Of course. Tomorrow it is! But I warn you, my dear, you won't get out of it so easily next time."

"Well, goodnight, everyone," she said, yawning once more. "I simply must get my beauty sleep. See you in the morning."

Pam climbed the stairs to her room. Once inside, she changed into shorts again. Then she turned out the light and waited.

The hours seemed to crawl by until the house was finally still. Pam had been afraid that she would fall asleep while waiting. At last, she was fairly certain that everyone had gone to bed. She tucked a small flashlight into her pocket and slipped out of her room.

She was afraid that Cameron might have guards on duty inside the house at night.

But she saw no one as she crept down to the main hall. Then she realized that the house itself would be protected by an alarm system. She began to relax a little. It was going to be easier than she'd thought.

The main hall was dark and silent. Pam slipped through the dining room to the large kitchen. There was a dim light burning over the stove. She could see the room without having to use her flashlight. She glanced about her and finally spotted Lehua's key ring hanging from a hook near the back door.

Pam tiptoed across the kitchen and lifted the key ring from the hook. She stuffed the key ring into her pocket so the keys would not jingle. Then she tiptoed from the kitchen back to the main hall.

It remained silent and empty. Still, Pam tried to stay in the shadows as she went.

When she reached the locked doors, she pulled out the key ring. She worked quickly but quietly, trying one key after another. At last she felt one of the keys turn in the lock. She tried the handle of the door and it opened!

Pam could hardly believe her good luck. Things were going so smoothly. If her luck held, she might have the information she needed very soon. Then tomorrow she'd find some excuse to get off the estate. Soon this would all be over and behind her.

Pam shut the doors quietly behind her. She used her flashlight and beamed it around the room. Cameron's big desk stood in front of the barred windows. Near it was a long table covered with papers. Behind the table was a bulletin board. Pam shined her light over the board. There were several maps pinned to it. She moved closer to study them.

One map showed the island of Oahu. Someone had marked on it with colored ink. She saw at once that part of the map was a military base. The next map was of the base itself. And there were pictures and diagrams on the board. Then Pam saw a paper that looked like a timetable. She leaned closer to read it. Sure enough, there were times and dates written on it.

This must be the information Dawson needed. But what exactly did it mean? As she tried to figure it out, the room was suddenly flooded with light. Pam cried out in surprise and whirled around. In the doorway stood Alexander Cameron and David Owens. Owens was holding a gun—and it was pointed right at Pam.

Cameron's face was white with anger. He turned to a small box on the wall by the door. He opened the box and pressed some buttons. With a sinking heart, Pam realized what it was. A silent alarm. When she had opened the door to the office, she had set it off. It probably had gone off in Cameron's bedroom. And she had thought that things were going so well.

As soon as he had turned off the alarm, Cameron turned on Pam. "So, Trish Norton, you're nothing but a dirty little spy!" he exclaimed.

Pam was startled. She had almost forgotten that Cameron thought of her as Trish.

"David was right," Cameron went on bitterly. "He said he thought you were just a little too nosy. But I didn't pay any attention. I should have listened!"

Pam said nothing.

"Who do you work for?" Owens asked Pam harshly. "How much do you know?"

"No one. I don't know anything. I was just looking for . . ."

"For information about my private army, right?" Cameron said harshly. "Don't try to make excuses, my dear. You've been caught red-handed."

Pam moaned, unable to hide her fear. Cameron heard her and laughed. "I'm sure you're working for someone in our government. It shows how right I am about what fools we have in Washington. Did they really think some bubbleheaded amateur could outsmart me?" He turned to Owens. "Get her out of here, and get rid of her."

"How, Mr. Cameron?" Owens asked.

Cameron stared at Pam for a long moment. Then he grinned slowly. "Take her out in my boat and drop her overboard. She can't swim. When her body washes up on shore, it will look like an accident."

Pam felt a sudden surge of hope. This could be her one way out.

"No!" she cried, shrinking back. "Please, Alexander, don't let me drown!"

Cameron laughed again. "Too bad, my dear. You should have thought of that before you tried to play secret agent. Okay, David, get going!"

"Wait!" Pam begged. "You don't have to kill me, Alexander. I really don't know what your plans are. You caught me before I could learn anything. Can't you just keep me here until—"

Cameron's loud laughter cut across her words. "Well, I'll *tell* you what my plans are, my dear. You won't be broadcasting them to anyone else. "I am going to *save* the United States."

Pam looked at him. There was a wild light shining in his eyes. "Save the United States from what?" she asked.

"From making a bigger fool of itself! All our leaders ever do is talk about peace. I'm sick of that wishy-washy nonsense. In two days, my army will take over that military base." He pointed to the map. "We'll take them by surprise, of course. Then, once we have control of the base, we'll use their weapons to attack our enemies."

"That will start a war," Pam exclaimed.

"Oh, no," Cameron said. "They, too, will be taken by surprise. It will be over before it really begins. And when the people of the United States realize how brilliant my plan is, they'll decide to follow me. No more talk about peace! We must show our strength. We must *destroy* our enemies."

He was completely mad, Pam saw. She glanced at Owens. "Do you feel the same way?" she asked him.

He nodded. "Of course. Mr. Cameron's ideas make a lot of sense to a great many people."

"But a lot of innocent people will be killed," Pam cried.

David shrugged. "There's always a price for everything," he said. "And speaking of paying a price, let's go. In a few hours it will be light. I don't want anyone to see us throwing you to the sharks!"

Suddenly Pam realized that her ability to swim might not save her after all. She would be in unknown waters. It was dark and dangerous. And there could very well be sharks out there. Still, it was the only chance she had.

A few minutes later Pam was in the back seat of the limousine. David Owens was sitting next to her with his gun pressed against her ribs. One of Cameron's guards was driving. The limousine purred through the quiet night toward the harbor. Pam had the same feeling now that she'd had at the beginning of the week. This was all a crazy dream. If she pinched herself, she'd wake up somewhere else. In the bank, maybe, or in the safety of the swimming pool. But she knew that the crazy dream had turned into a nightmare. Pinching herself wouldn't help.

When they reached the dock, David pulled Pam from the car and shoved her toward Cameron's boat. "Don't make a sound," he told her. "I wouldn't think twice about pulling this trigger."

The guard started the engine and the boat headed for the mouth of the harbor. "How far out do you want to go?" the guard asked Owens.

"Just beyond the reef, into the channel," he said. "That's far enough."

Once the boat was out of the smooth waters of the harbor, the ocean became choppy. Pam could hear the waves crashing against the reefs. She shivered. The reefs were made of coral, and they were knife sharp. Another danger she would have to face.

Then the guard cut the engine. The boat pitched around in the rough water. "Throw her over!" Owens yelled.

"You heard the man," the guard said, pushing Pam toward the side of the boat. "This is as far as you go, lady!"

"No!" Pam screamed, fighting to break away from him. Then she felt the strong hands of the guard picking her up. He lifted her up and over the side. A second later she was falling. And then the dark waters closed over her head.

Pam fought her way to the surface, kicking off her shoes as she went. When she broke above the water, she saw the lights of the boat moving away. The guard had wasted no time in starting the engine and heading home. Pam watched the lights disappear. She knew she had to swim in the same direction. Somewhere ahead of her was the mouth of the harbor. If only she could get out of the rough currents of the channel and get past the reef. But already she could feel the water carrying her from the spot where she'd been thrown in.

Then she remembered the earring! Frank Dawson had told her to use it if her life were in danger. She couldn't think of a better situation than this one. She rolled onto her back and floated while she pressed the pearl in the earring as Dawson had told her.

She hoped that the water hadn't damaged the tiny transmitter. And she hoped that Dawson would pick up the signal and get to her in time. She wished she'd remembered it before now. But there was no use in wishing. She rolled over and began to swim again.

Suddenly a swell lifted her and pushed her forward. She slammed into the coral reef. Pain cut through her body. At first she couldn't move. The pain was so bad, she was almost sick with it. She felt herself sucked back into the current. She knew that the next swell would smash her against the sharp coral again. She would be beaten to death on the reef if she didn't do something to save herself.

This time when Pam felt the water lift her, she was ready. She was slammed into the reef a second time, but this time she grabbed a spike of coral that jutted up from the reef. The sharp points of the coral cut into her hands, but she was able to hold on anyway.

Luckily, the top of the reef was above the water. Pam let the next wave lift her over the top. The reef was like a wide ledge. It was slippery with seaweed, but Pam managed to roll across it. She slipped into the water on the harbor side.

Here the water was a little quieter. If she could just hang onto those rocks, she could wait for Frank Dawson to rescue her. She reached up to make sure the earring was still in place. To her horror, her fingertips touched only bare skin. The earring must have been knocked off when she'd been thrown against the reef. Frank Dawson would not be able to trace her now. She was on her own.

For a moment, Pam wanted to cry. She was tired and in a lot of pain. She could probably hang on to these rocks for a few hours more and hope for someone to find her. But then she remembered Cameron's plans! She had to try and get that information to Frank Dawson as fast as she could.

Pam felt a great sense of despair. But she forced herself to leave the safety of the rocks and begin swimming again. Then her old swimming trick came back to her. The familiar words began to go round and round in her head. *Don't give up! You're almost there!* This time she was not in a safe, familiar pool. And there was no edge to reach for if she got too tired. There was no coach to offer encouragement. She could only count on herself.

"You wanted to be a long-distance swimmer," she told herself grimly. "So don't give up! You're almost there!"

Pam lost track of how long she was in the water. Gradually, her mind went blank and her body went numb. She knew she just could not make it. She was too tired. Her muscles refused to work. Soon she would probably start to sink. The waters would close over her. She would drown. This is it, she thought bitterly. This is the end. The game was too dangerous for her. She had lost the race after all.

Suddenly she felt strong hands lifting her from the water. They pulled her into a boat. The bright beam of a flashlight was turned onto her face. It nearly blinded her. She winced and turned away.

"She's alive!" she heard someone say. It was a voice she knew—Frank Dawson's!

Later, wrapped in warm blankets and sipping hot coffee, Pam was able to tell Dawson everything he needed to know.

"You did it, Pam," he said with a big grin. "We'll be able to stop Cameron in time."

She smiled weakly. "How did you find me?" she asked. "I lost the earring and I thought that was it!"

"We got your signal just long enough to know about where you were," Dawson said. "But it's a good thing you're such a fine swimmer."

Pam nodded. She felt good inside. She was sore and tired, but she felt better than she'd ever felt before. She'd found the nerve to play a dangerous game. And in the end, she'd won.